ESPECIALLY FOR

....

FROM

....

DATE

....

Start with a
PRAYER

A GUIDED JOURNAL FOR YOUR BEST DAY

BARBOUR BOOKS
An Imprint of Barbour Publishing, Inc.

© 2020 by Barbour Publishing, Inc.

ISBN 978-1-64352-446-7

Written and compiled by JoAnne Simmons.

Published by Barbour Books, an imprint of Barbour Publishing, Inc., 1810 Barbour Drive, Uhrichsville, Ohio 44683, www.barbourbooks.com

Our mission is to inspire the world with the life-changing message of the Bible.

 Member of the Evangelical Christian Publishers Association

Printed in China.

Introduction

Each new day is a gift from God and an opportunity to grow in your relationship with Him—and no relationship can grow without good communication! Let this journal encourage you into a deeper prayer life and closer fellowship with your heavenly Father who loves you infinitely and indescribably.

The devotional prayers within this book, based on passages straight from God's Word, are simply starting points to inspire more prayer of your own. After reading and praying, you can record your personal prayers, lists of requests, and answers to prayer in the pages that follow. And as you journal in response to the prompts, you can ponder and reflect on what God is teaching you about relationship with Him and how to live out your faith so that others might know and love Him too.

In the end, you'll have created a beautiful keepsake to remind you of all the ways you've grown and the many gifts God gives you. It's such a powerful, faith-building blessing to look back and see how God is working in your life and in the lives of your loved ones.

Start each day with a prayer—and then delight in where God leads you!

THIS IS THE DAY
THE LORD HAS MADE.
WE WILL REJOICE
AND BE GLAD IN IT.

PSALM 118:24 NLT

START WITH A PRAYER

Heavenly Father, I rejoice because You have given me this day. You are the Giver of life on earth and You are the Giver of eternal life in the Kingdom You are preparing. I praise You for saving me from my sin. Thank You for reconciling me to You through Your Son, Jesus Christ. I want to know You and serve You better and better each new day. Amen.

....

....

....

....

....

....

....

....

....

....

....

....

Anyone who belongs to Christ has become a new person.
The old life is gone; a new life has begun! And all of this is
a gift from God, who brought us back to himself through
Christ. And God has given us this task of reconciling people
to him. For God was in Christ, reconciling the world to himself,
no longer counting people's sins against them. And he
gave us this wonderful message of reconciliation.
2 CORINTHIANS 5:17–19 NLT

MY PRAYER FOR TODAY. . .

Share the details of when and how you personally accepted Jesus Christ as your Savior. How did that decision begin a new life and prayer life for you?

....

....

....

....

....

....

....

....

....

....

....

....

....

....

....

....

....

....

For God made Christ, who never sinned, to be the offering for our sin, so that we could be made right with God through Christ.
2 CORINTHIANS 5:21 NLT

ANSWERS TO PRAYER. . .

MY PRAYER LIST. . .

....

....

....

....

....

....

....

....

....

....

....

....

....

....

....

....

*I have written this to you who believe in the name of the
Son of God, so that you may know you have eternal life.
And we are confident that he hears us whenever
we ask for anything that pleases him.*

1 JOHN 5:13–14 NLT

START WITH A PRAYER

Heavenly Father, please help me to remember every day that my actions here on earth have an impact on my eternal life. No matter my circumstances, I am Your child. I want to obey and please You through every blessing and through every trial. Today, please guide me in the good things You have planned for me, all for Your glory. Amen.

....

....

....

....

....

....

....

....

....

....

....

....

....

We are always confident and know that as long as we are at home in the body we are away from the Lord. For we live by faith, not by sight. We are confident, I say, and would prefer to be away from the body and at home with the Lord. So we make it our goal to please him, whether we are at home in the body or away from it. For we must all appear before the judgment seat of Christ, so that each of us may receive what is due us for the things done while in the body, whether good or bad.

2 CORINTHIANS 5:6–10 NIV

My PRAYER FOR TODAY. . .

If you focus each morning on living by faith and not sight, remembering you will one day give an account before Christ of your life on earth, how will that affect the course and purpose of your day? How will you communicate with God throughout each day?

....

....

....

....

....

....

....

....

....

....

....

....

....

....

....

Nothing in all creation is hidden from God's sight.
Everything is uncovered and laid bare before the
eyes of him to whom we must give account.
HEBREWS 4:13 NIV

ANSWERS TO PRAYER. . .

MY PRAYER LIST. . .

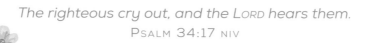

The righteous cry out, and the Lord hears them.
PSALM 34:17 NIV

START WiTH A PRAYER

Heavenly Father, please refresh and renew my trust in You on this new day. You have proven Yourself time and time again, and I have every reason to believe You will continue to do so today and in the future. Strengthen my whole heart with great faith in You. I submit all of my ways and all of my mind to You, God. Please lead me along the straight paths You have laid out for me. Amen.

....

....

....

....

....

....

....

....

....

....

....

....

....

....

Trust in the Lord with all your heart and lean not on your own understanding; in all your ways submit to him, and he will make your paths straight.
PROVERBS 3:5–6 NIV

MY PRAYER FOR TODAY. . .

In what ways has God shown you not to lean on your own understanding? Share about a time when He straightened the crooked paths of your life, requiring you to trust and submit everything completely to Him. Praise Him as you remember this time.

....

....

....

....

....

....

....

....

....

....

....

....

....

....

Commit your way to the LORD;
trust in him, and he will act.
PSALM 37:5 ESV

ANSWERS TO PRAYER. . .

MY PRAYER LiST. . .

"If you abide in me, and my words abide in you,
ask whatever you wish, and it will be done for you."
JOHN 15:7 ESV

START WITH A PRAYER

Heavenly Father, sometimes I wake up with very little heart to face the day, but Your Word urges me to never lose heart. Remind me that even though everything in this fallen world—including me—is wasting away on the outside, You are renewing my eternal soul day by day. Please help me to keep my focus on the unseen things You are doing. Remind me how temporary this world and its troubles are, and fill me with joy and expectation for Your coming glory. Amen.

*Therefore we do not lose heart. Though outwardly we
are wasting away, yet inwardly we are being renewed day
by day. For our light and momentary troubles are achieving
for us an eternal glory that far outweighs them all.
So we fix our eyes not on what is seen, but on what is unseen,
since what is seen is temporary, but what is unseen is eternal.*

2 CORINTHIANS 4:16–18 NIV

MY PRAYER FOR TODAY. . .

What does it look like to fix your eyes on what is unseen? Describe what God has shown you when you've focused on eternal rather than temporal things.

....
....
....
....
....
....
....
....
....
....
....
....
....
....
....
....

*Now faith is confidence in what we hope for
and assurance about what we do not see.*
HEBREWS 11:1 NIV

ANSWERS TO PRAYER. . .

MY PRAYER LiST. . .

_____

_____

_____

_____

_____

_____

_____

_____

_____

_____

_____

_____

_____

_____

_____

_____

_____

_____

_____

_____

_____

Continue steadfastly in prayer,
being watchful in it with thanksgiving.
COLOSSIANS 4:2 ESV

START WITH A PRAYER

Heavenly Father, please remind me this new day and every day that I live in the shelter of You, the Most High. I find rest in Your shadow, Almighty One. You are my refuge and my safety. You are my God, and I trust You. You rescue me from every form of evil in this world. You cover me and shelter me. I am protected by Your faithful promises. Oh, how grateful I am to be Your child! Amen.

Those who live in the shelter of the Most High will find rest in the shadow of the Almighty. This I declare about the Lord: He alone is my refuge, my place of safety; he is my God, and I trust him. For he will rescue you from every trap and protect you from deadly disease. He will cover you with his feathers. He will shelter you with his wings. His faithful promises are your armor and protection.
PSALM 91:1–4 NLT

MY PRAYER FOR TODAY. . .

Write about a scary experience when God clearly showed Himself as your rescuer and protector. What did you do, how did you pray, and how did God answer?

....

....

....

....

....

....

....

....

....

....

....

....

....

....

....

....

....

....

The Lord says, "I will rescue those who love me. I will protect those who trust in my name. When they call on me, I will answer; I will be with them in trouble. I will rescue and honor them. I will reward them with a long life and give them my salvation."
Psalm 91:14–16 NLT

ANSWERS TO PRAYER. . .

MY PRAYER LIST. . .

In my distress I called upon the LORD; to my
God I cried for help. From his temple he heard
my voice, and my cry to him reached his ears.

PSALM 18:6 ESV

START WITH A PRAYER

Heavenly Father, just like I threw off the covers to get out of bed this morning, help me to throw off everything that keeps me from growing closer to You. I want to rid my life of sin, which trips me up and keeps me from doing the good things You have planned for me. I want to run the race You have marked for me and put all my focus on pleasing You until I fall into Your loving arms at the finish line. Amen.

Since we are surrounded by such a great cloud of witnesses, let us throw off everything that hinders and the sin that so easily entangles. And let us run with perseverance the race marked out for us, fixing our eyes on Jesus, the pioneer and perfecter of faith.
HEBREWS 12:1–2 NIV

My PRAYER FOR TODAY. . .

Is there sin tripping you up today, keeping you from running the race God has for you? List the sins you are struggling with, confessing them to God and asking for His grace to cover them and banish them from your life.

....

....

....

....

....

....

....

....

....

....

....

....

....

....

....

....

*If we confess our sins, he is faithful and just to forgive
us our sins and to cleanse us from all unrighteousness.*
1 JOHN 1:9 ESV

ANSWERS TO PRAYER. . .

MY PRAYER LiST. . .

Therefore, confess your sins to one another and pray
for one another, that you may be healed. The prayer of
a righteous person has great power as it is working.

JAMES 5:16 ESV

START WITH A PRAYER

Heavenly Father, the world seems to grow increasingly darker with sin, and that can feel so discouraging. Please remind me that You sent Your Son as the Light of the World. Jesus makes my path through this world clear, step by step, day by day. Your light leads to life, no matter how the darkness falls around me. Please help me to live in Your light and constantly shine it for others to see and follow You too. Amen.

....

....

....

....

....

....

....

....

....

....

....

....

....

....

Jesus spoke to the people once more and said, "I am the light of the world. If you follow me, you won't have to walk in darkness, because you will have the light that leads to life."

JOHN 8:12 NLT

MY PRAYER FOR TODAY. . .

What specific darkness do you see spreading around you? How are you praying against it and shining God's light to pierce it?

In the beginning was the Word, and the Word was with God, and the Word was God. He was with God in the beginning. Through him all things were made; without him nothing was made that has been made. In him was life, and that life was the light of all mankind. The light shines in the darkness, and the darkness has not overcome it.

JOHN 1:1–5 NIV

ANSWERS TO PRAYER. . .

MY PRAYER LiST. . .

_You, Lord, keep my lamp burning; my God turns my
darkness into light. With your help I can advance
against a troop; with my God I can scale a wall._
PSALM 18:28–29 NIV

START WITH A PRAYER

Heavenly Father, sometimes I begin my day remembering ways I have suffered in the past or focusing too much on what I am suffering right now. Despite it all though, I will continue to hope in You, loving God! You give new mercy and care every single morning, and You are so faithful to me even when I am unfaithful to You. There is no pain or wound in my life or my heart so great that You cannot comfort and heal. I trust You to always love and provide for me. Amen.

....

....

....

....

....

....

....

....

....

....

....

....

*The thought of my suffering and homelessness is bitter beyond words. I will never forget this awful time, as I grieve over my loss. Yet I still dare to hope when I remember this: The faithful love of the L*ORD *never ends! His mercies never cease. Great is his faithfulness; his mercies begin afresh each morning. I say to myself, "The L*ORD *is my inheritance; therefore, I will hope in him!"*
LAMENTATIONS 3:19–24 NLT

MY PRAYER FOR TODAY. . .

Describe a time when you experienced God's mercy in the midst of suffering and a time when you experienced total healing and restoration after suffering. Praise Him as you remember His care.

....

....

....

....

....

....

....

....

....

....

....

....

....

....

....

....

In his kindness God called you to share in his eternal glory by means of Christ Jesus. So after you have suffered a little while, he will restore, support, and strengthen you, and he will place you on a firm foundation. All power to him forever! Amen.
1 PETER 5:10–11 NLT

ANSWERS TO PRAYER. . .

MY PRAYER LiST. . .

....

....

....

....

....

....

....

....

....

....

....

....

....

....

....

....

....

*But I will call on God, and the Lord will rescue
me. Morning, noon, and night I cry out in my
distress, and the Lord hears my voice.*
PSALM 55:16–17 NLT

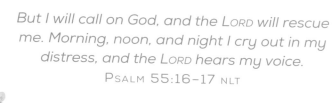

START WITH A PRAYER

Heavenly Father, I want each of my days to be filled with praise to You, not just through my words and songs but in everything I do. Help me to remember that with every task and action—and even every thought—I can bring glory to You. Work in and through me, God. Fill me up with Your love and truth, and help me proclaim Your greatness to those around me. Focus my mind constantly on who You are, all You have done, and all You are doing. Amen.

Give thanks to the Lord and proclaim his greatness. Let the whole world know what he has done. Sing to him; yes, sing his praises. Tell everyone about his wonderful deeds. Exult in his holy name; rejoice, you who worship the Lord. Search for the Lord and for his strength; continually seek him. Remember the wonders he has performed, his miracles, and the rulings he has given, you children of his servant Israel, you descendants of Jacob, his chosen ones.

1 Chronicles 16:8–13 NLT

MY PRAYER FOR TODAY. . .

List ways you are proclaiming God's greatness with your life and ways you can do even more.

....

....

....

....

....

....

....

....

....

....

....

....

....

....

....

Sing to the LORD, praise his name; proclaim his salvation day after day. Declare his glory among the nations, his marvelous deeds among all peoples.
PSALM 96:2-3 NIV

ANSWERS TO PRAYER. . .

MY PRAYER LIST. . .

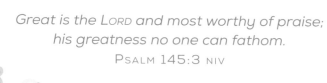

Great is the LORD and most worthy of praise;
his greatness no one can fathom.
PSALM 145:3 NIV

START WITH A PRAYER

Heavenly Father, I come to You today weary and burdened, like Your Word describes. I desperately need You to give me the supernatural kind of rest only You can provide. Remind me that You don't want me to carry heavy burdens. Help me to give them up, Father. Please help me to focus only on the good things You want me to do. Align my priorities with Your will and Your ways. Amen.

....

....

....

....

....

....

....

....

....

....

....

....

....

"Come to me, all you who are weary and burdened, and I will give you rest. Take my yoke upon you and learn from me, for I am gentle and humble in heart, and you will find rest for your souls. For my yoke is easy and my burden is light."
MATTHEW 11:28–30 NIV

MY PRAYER FOR TODAY. . .

What burdens are exhausting you in your life? As you seek to rest in God's love and care, what is He calling you to do about your burdens?

....

....

....

....

....

....

....

....

....

....

....

....

....

....

....

....

....

Cast all your anxiety on him because he cares for you.
1 PETER 5:7 NIV

ANSWERS TO PRAYER. . .

MY PRAYER LIST. . .

In peace I will both lie down and sleep;
for you alone, O Lord, make me dwell in safety.
Psalm 4:8 esv

START WITH A PRAYER

Heavenly Father, I so easily forget how great and mighty You are. Please forgive me, for there is nothing and no one comparable to You. I am blessed to be called Your child and privileged to serve You. As I begin a new day, fill me with absolute awe of You, my everlasting God. I give this day and every day of my life to You. All my hope and strength are in You. Amen.

*Do you not know? Have you not heard? The L*ORD *is the everlasting God, the Creator of the ends of the earth. He will not grow tired or weary, and his understanding no one can fathom. He gives strength to the weary and increases the power of the weak. Even youths grow tired and weary, and young men stumble and fall; but those who hope in the L*ORD *will renew their strength. They will soar on wings like eagles; they will run and not grow weary, they will walk and not be faint.*
ISAIAH 40:28–31 NIV

MY PRAYER FOR TODAY. . .

Describe specific ways God has been filling you with awe of Him lately.

....

....

....

....

....

....

....

....

....

....

....

....

....

....

....

....

....

*The LORD your God is God of gods and Lord
of lords, the great God, mighty and awesome.*
DEUTERONOMY 10:17 NIV

ANSWERS TO PRAYER. . .

....
....
....
....
....
....
....
....
....
....
....
....
....
....
....
....
....
....
....
....
....
....

MY PRAYER LIST. . .

....
....
....
....
....
....
....
....
....
....
....
....
....
....
....
....
....

*"Blessed be your glorious name, and may it be exalted
above all blessing and praise. You alone are the LORD.
You made the heavens, even the highest heavens, and all
their starry host, the earth and all that is on it, the seas
and all that is in them. You give life to everything,
and the multitudes of heaven worship you."*
NEHEMIAH 9:5–6 NIV

START WITH A PRAYER

Heavenly Father, You are my Master, and I want to be used for every good work You have for me. Help me to keep myself pure, staying far away from sinful actions, thoughts, words, influences, and attitudes. I want my life to be clean and available to You so that I can honor You and make You known! There is no better purpose in life. I love You and long to obey You. Amen.

....

....

....

....

....

....

....

....

....

....

....

....

....

In a wealthy home some utensils are made of gold and silver, and some are made of wood and clay. The expensive utensils are used for special occasions, and the cheap ones are for everyday use. If you keep yourself pure, you will be a special utensil for honorable use. Your life will be clean, and you will be ready for the Master to use you for every good work.
2 Timothy 2:20–21 nlt

MY PRAYER FOR TODAY. . .

Describe how you've seen God use your life honorably, and praise Him for those opportunities. Then ask God what areas of your life need some cleanup work so that you may be ready for Him to use you even more.

....

....

....

....

....

....

....

....

....

....

....

....

....

....

....

....

Flee the evil desires of youth and pursue righteousness,
faith, love and peace, along with those who
call on the Lord out of a pure heart.
2 TIMOTHY 2:22 NIV

ANSWERS TO PRAYER. . .

my PRAYER LiST. . .

Create in me a clean heart, O God,
and renew a right spirit within me.
PSALM 51:10 ESV

START WITH A PRAYER

Heavenly Father, some days I feel like trouble is coming into my life from every single direction. When it threatens to completely overwhelm me, remind me that You will never let it crush me or destroy me or drive me to despair. You will never abandon me in the midst of it. When I suffer, remind me I share in the suffering of Your Son, Jesus. As I depend on You for help with hardship, You make Jesus' life and love known through me. Amen.

....

....

....

....

....

....

....

....

....

....

....

....

....

....

We are pressed on every side by troubles, but we are not crushed. We are perplexed, but not driven to despair. We are hunted down, but never abandoned by God. We get knocked down, but we are not destroyed. Through suffering, our bodies continue to share in the death of Jesus so that the life of Jesus may also be seen in our bodies.

2 Corinthians 4:8–10 NLT

MY PRAYER FOR TODAY. . .

What troubles are pressing in on you these days? As you ask God for help, how do you see Him working to not let those troubles destroy you? How do you see Him working to share the life and love of Jesus in the midst of them?

....

....

....

....

....

....

....

....

....

....

....

....

....

....

....

....

"In this world you will have trouble.
But take heart! I have overcome the world."
JOHN 16:33 NIV

ANSWERS TO PRAYER. . .

MY PRAYER LiST. . .

The righteous person may have many troubles,
but the Lord delivers him from them all.
PSALM 34:19 NIV

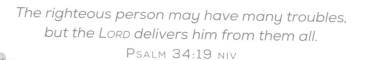

START WITH A PRAYER

Heavenly Father, I want to learn from the way Jesus taught us to pray. He honored and praised You. He longed for Your Kingdom to come and Your will to be done on earth as it is in heaven. He asked for daily needs to be met. He taught us to seek forgiveness and to be willing to forgive others. He taught us to pray to avoid sin and temptation and to be delivered from evil. Please remind me of Your Son's perfect way of prayer every time I speak to You, dear Father. Amen.

*"This, then, is how you should pray:
'Our Father in heaven, hallowed be your name, your kingdom
come, your will be done, on earth as it is in heaven.
Give us today our daily bread. And forgive us our debts,
as we also have forgiven our debtors. And lead us not
into temptation, but deliver us from the evil one.'"*
MATTHEW 6:9–13 NIV

MY PRAYER FOR TODAY. . .

Describe how you have grown in your prayer life. In what ways could you continue to learn and grow?

....
....
....
....
....
....
....
....
....
....
....
....
....
....
....
....
....

*"Call to me and I will answer you and tell you
great and unsearchable things you do not know."*
JEREMIAH 33:3 NIV

ANSWERS TO PRAYER. . .

MY PRAYER LIST. . .

And pray in the Spirit on all occasions with all kinds
of prayers and requests. With this in mind, be alert
and always keep on praying for all the Lord's people.
EPHESIANS 6:18 NIV

START WITH A PRAYER

Heavenly Father, too often life's trials make me feel like giving up. Please assure me that You are working in the middle of them to develop my character exactly as You have planned. I surrender to You and the work You are doing in my life through any kind of struggle and pain. I trust that You dearly love me and are working out Your best for me in all things. Amen.

*We can rejoice, too, when we run into problems and trials,
for we know that they help us develop endurance. And endurance
develops strength of character, and character strengthens
our confident hope of salvation. And this hope will not lead to
disappointment. For we know how dearly God loves us, because
he has given us the Holy Spirit to fill our hearts with his love.*
ROMANS 5:3–5 NLT

START WITH A PRAYER

Heavenly Father, I know many people who are not in relationship with You through the Mediator You sent us, Jesus Christ. Please help these dear people with all of their needs, and draw them close to You. I pray they come to believe in Your Son as the one and only Way, Truth, and Life. I pray they accept Jesus Christ as the Savior of their sins and their only hope for eternal life. Thank You for the privilege of knowing and praying for these people. Amen.

....

....

....

....

....

....

....

....

....

....

....

....

I urge you, first of all, to pray for all people. Ask God to help them; intercede on their behalf, and give thanks for them. Pray this way for kings and all who are in authority so that we can live peaceful and quiet lives marked by godliness and dignity. This is good and pleases God our Savior, who wants everyone to be saved and to understand the truth. For, There is one God and one Mediator who can reconcile God and humanity—the man Christ Jesus. He gave his life to purchase freedom for everyone.

1 TIMOTHY 2:1-6 NLT

MY PRAYER FOR TODAY. . .

Who are the specific people you feel called to pray regularly for to come to know Christ as Savior? How might you support those people on a daily basis?

....

....

....

....

....

....

....

....

....

....

....

....

....

....

....

....

Jesus said to him, "I am the way, and the truth, and the life. No one comes to the Father except through me."
JOHN 14:6 ESV

ANSWERS TO PRAYER. . .

my PRAYER LIST. . .

....
....
....
....
....
....
....
....
....
....
....
....
....
....
....
....
....
....

*If you declare with your mouth, "Jesus is Lord," and believe
in your heart that God raised him from the dead, you will
be saved. For it is with your heart that you believe and
are justified, and it is with your mouth that you
profess your faith and are saved.*
ROMANS 10:9–10 NIV

START WITH A PRAYER

Heavenly Father, I need Your wisdom in every area of my life. You promise in Your Word to give it, and I believe You. Help me to apply the wisdom You are giving to the challenging situations I'm in the middle of and the tough decisions I need to make—and simply in my day-to-day life as I strive to serve and glorify You. Help me to point others to You and Your perfect wisdom too. Amen.

If you need wisdom, ask our generous God, and he will give it to you. He will not rebuke you for asking. But when you ask him, be sure that your faith is in God alone. Do not waver, for a person with divided loyalty is as unsettled as a wave of the sea that is blown and tossed by the wind. Such people should not expect to receive anything from the Lord. Their loyalty is divided between God and the world, and they are unstable in everything they do.

JAMES 1:5–8 NLT

MY PRAYER FOR TODAY. . .

....

....

....

....

....

....

....

....

....

....

....

....

....

....

....

....

....

....

....

....

What challenges and decisions are you facing in your life right now that you need God's wisdom for? How are you seeking His wisdom?

Look carefully then how you walk, not as unwise but as wise, making the best use of the time, because the days are evil. Therefore do not be foolish, but understand what the will of the Lord is.
EPHESIANS 5:15–17 ESV

ANSWERS TO PRAYER. . .

MY PRAYER LIST. . .

*For the LORD gives wisdom; from his mouth
come knowledge and understanding.*
PROVERBS 2:6 NIV

START WITH A PRAYER

Heavenly Father, Your Word tells me not to worry, but I still struggle with it far too often. Please help me to turn each worry that pops into my mind into a prayer instead, remembering You are sovereign and good and are working in every situation and need. When worries threaten to consume me, please fix my thoughts on trusting and praising You. There is absolutely nothing You cannot handle. Amen.

....

....

....

....

....

....

....

....

....

....

....

....

"I tell you, do not worry about your life, what you will eat or drink; or about your body, what you will wear. Is not life more than food, and the body more than clothes? Look at the birds of the air; they do not sow or reap or store away in barns, and yet your heavenly Father feeds them. Are you not much more valuable than they? Can any one of you by worrying add a single hour to your life?"

MATTHEW 6:25–27 NIV

MY PRAYER FOR TODAY. . .

_____
_____
_____
_____
_____
_____
_____
_____
_____
_____
_____
_____
_____
_____
_____
_____
_____
_____
_____
_____
_____
_____

List your current worries; beside them, list specific qualities of God and praises to Him that help you remember He will provide for every need and sustain you through every circumstance.

....

....

....

....

....

....

....

....

....

....

....

....

....

"Do not worry, saying, 'What shall we eat?' or 'What shall we drink?' or 'What shall we wear?' For the pagans run after all these things, and your heavenly Father knows that you need them. But seek first his kingdom and his righteousness, and all these things will be given to you as well. Therefore do not worry about tomorrow, for tomorrow will worry about itself. Each day has enough trouble of its own."
MATTHEW 6:31–34 NIV

ANSWERS TO PRAYER. . .

MY PRAYER LIST. . .

Give your burdens to the LORD,
and he will take care of you.
PSALM 55:22 NLT

START WITH A PRAYER

Heavenly Father, sometimes I feel like I don't have much to offer You, especially when I take my eyes off You and spend too much time comparing myself to others. Forgive me. Every single gift I have—whether it is a quality or talent, money or a material possession—ultimately comes from You. So no matter how big or small my gifts seem, I offer everything back for Your use—to build Your Kingdom, to share Your truth and love, and to give You all the glory. I know You can multiply anything I give into so much more. Amen.

Jesus sat down near the collection box in the Temple and watched as the crowds dropped in their money. Many rich people put in large amounts. Then a poor widow came and dropped in two small coins. Jesus called his disciples to him and said, "I tell you the truth, this poor widow has given more than all the others who are making contributions. For they gave a tiny part of their surplus, but she, poor as she is, has given everything she had to live on."

MARK 12:41–44 NLT

MY PRAYER FOR TODAY. . .

Do you ever struggle with being generous? How can prayer help you find more joy in sharing the gifts God has given you?

....

....

....

....

....

....

....

....

....

....

....

....

....

Remember this: Whoever sows sparingly will also reap sparingly, and whoever sows generously will also reap generously. Each of you should give what you have decided in your heart to give, not reluctantly or under compulsion, for God loves a cheerful giver. And God is able to bless you abundantly, so that in all things at all times, having all that you need, you will abound in every good work.
2 CORINTHIANS 9:6–8 NIV

ANSWERS TO PRAYER. . .

MY PRAYER LIST. . .

"Give, and it will be given to you. Good measure, pressed down, shaken together, running over, will be put into your lap. For with the measure you use it will be measured back to you."

LUKE 6:38 ESV

START WITH A PRAYER

Heavenly Father, I pray that from Your glorious, unlimited resources You will empower me with inner strength through Your Spirit. I want Christ to be comfortably at home in my heart as I trust in Him. I want strong roots growing down deep into Your incredible love for me. I cannot ever fully understand it here on earth, but every day I want to understand more and more of how wide, long, high, and deep Your love is. What an unfathomable honor and blessing it is to be Your child! Amen.

When I think of all this, I fall to my knees and pray to the Father, the Creator of everything in heaven and on earth. I pray that from his glorious, unlimited resources he will empower you with inner strength through his Spirit. Then Christ will make his home in your hearts as you trust in him. Your roots will grow down into God's love and keep you strong. And may you have the power to understand, as all God's people should, how wide, how long, how high, and how deep his love is.

EPHESIANS 3:14–18 NLT

MY PRAYER FOR TODAY. . .

What does it mean to have roots growing deep into God's love? How has prayer helped you grow in your understanding of God's love for you?

....

....

....

....

....

....

....

....

....

....

....

....

....

....

....

....

....

....

May you experience the love of Christ, though it is too great to understand fully. Then you will be made complete with all the fullness of life and power that comes from God.
EPHESIANS 3:19 NLT

ANSWERS TO PRAYER. . .

MY PRAYER LIST. . .

Now all glory to God, who is able, through his mighty power at work within us, to accomplish infinitely more than we might ask or think. Glory to him in the church and in Christ Jesus through all generations forever and ever! Amen.
EPHESIANS 3:20–21 NLT

START WITH A PRAYER

Heavenly Father, help me to constantly turn away from evil and sin. Because Your Son offered me the way to be Your child, I know that You will always be my Father—no matter what. But I know that sin in my life can have negative effects on our relationship and our communication. I always want to be in close fellowship with You, dear Father. Forgive me for my sin. Please cover it with Your amazing grace. Thank You, my God and Savior! Amen.

....

....

....

....

....

....

....

....

....

....

....

....

....

....

Come, my children, and listen to me, and I will teach you to fear the Lord. Does anyone want to live a life that is long and prosperous? Then keep your tongue from speaking evil and your lips from telling lies! Turn away from evil and do good. Search for peace, and work to maintain it. The eyes of the Lord watch over those who do right; his ears are open to their cries for help. But the Lord turns his face against those who do evil; he will erase their memory from the earth.
PSALM 34:11–16 NLT

MY PRAYER FOR TODAY. . .

What personal sins or struggles might be affecting your prayer life and keeping you from close fellowship with your loving heavenly Father? What do you need to do to turn from them?

....

....

....

....

....

....

....

....

....

....

....

....

....

....

....

Come and listen, all you who fear God, and I will tell you what he did for me. For I cried out to him for help, praising him as I spoke. If I had not confessed the sin in my heart, the Lord would not have listened. But God did listen! He paid attention to my prayer. Praise God, who did not ignore my prayer or withdraw his unfailing love from me.
PSALM 66:16–20 NLT

ANSWERS TO PRAYER. . .

my PRAYER LiST. . .

....

....

....

....

....

....

....

....

....

....

....

....

....

....

....

....

....

....

Well then, should we keep on sinning so that God
can show us more and more of his wonderful
grace? Of course not! Since we have died to sin,
how can we continue to live in it?
ROMANS 6:1–2 NLT

START WITH A PRAYER

Heavenly Father, please remind me every day that spiritual battle is a real thing. Unseen enemy forces are trying to fight against every good thing You do. They attack Your people, trying to destroy them, and they try to keep people from turning away from sin and accepting You as Savior. Prepare me each day with Your holy armor to stand firm and fight against this evil, I pray. Amen.

....

....

....

....

....

....

....

....

....

....

....

....

....

....

We are not fighting against flesh-and-blood enemies, but against evil rulers and authorities of the unseen world, against mighty powers in this dark world, and against evil spirits in the heavenly places. Therefore, put on every piece of God's armor so you will be able to resist the enemy in the time of evil. Then after the battle you will still be standing firm. Stand your ground, putting on the belt of truth and the body armor of God's righteousness. For shoes, put on the peace that comes from the Good News so that you will be fully prepared. In addition to all of these, hold up the shield of faith to stop the fiery arrows of the devil. Put on salvation as your helmet, and take the sword of the Spirit, which is the word of God.

EPHESIANS 6:12–17 NLT

My PRAYER FOR TODAY. . .

Have you ever felt attacked by evil spirits? Describe the experience and how God helped you stand firm and fight against them.

....

....

....

....

....

....

....

....

....

....

....

....

....

....

....

....

....

....

*Stay alert! Watch out for your great enemy, the devil.
He prowls around like a roaring lion, looking for someone to
devour. Stand firm against him, and be strong in your faith.*
1 PETER 5:8–9 NLT

ANSWERS TO PRAYER. . .

MY PRAYER LIST. . .

....
....
....
....
....
....
....
....
....
....
....
....
....
....
....
....
....
....
....
....
....
....

Submit yourselves, then, to God.
Resist the devil, and he will flee from you.
JAMES 4:7 NIV

START WITH A PRAYER

Heavenly Father, as I read Your Word and listen to teachings of Your Word, please help what I'm learning to stick in my mind and in my heart. Help me recall scripture exactly when I need it. I want to use it to keep me from sinning against You. I want to love and obey all You have said in Your Word and live it out to help others know and love You too. Amen.

I have hidden your word in my heart, that I might not sin against you. I praise you, O LORD; teach me your decrees. I have recited aloud all the regulations you have given us. I have rejoiced in your laws as much as in riches. I will study your commandments and reflect on your ways. I will delight in your decrees and not forget your word. Be good to your servant, that I may live and obey your word. Open my eyes to see the wonderful truths in your instructions.
PSALM 119:11–18 NLT

MY PRAYER FOR TODAY. . .

Jot down all the scriptures you know by heart. Then describe a time God brought a specific scripture to mind exactly when you needed it most.

....

....

....

....

....

....

....

....

....

....

....

....

....

....

....

....

....

....

....

....

....

....

*All Scripture is breathed out by God
and profitable for teaching, for reproof,
for correction, and for training in righteousness.*
2 Timothy 3:16 esv

ANSWERS TO PRAYER. . .

....

....

....

....

....

....

....

....

....

....

....

....

....

....

....

....

....

....

....

....

....

....

....

MY PRAYER LiST. . .

_Joyful are people of integrity, who follow the
instructions of the Lord. Joyful are those who obey
his laws and search for him with all their hearts._
Psalm 119:1-2 nlt

START WITH A PRAYER

Heavenly Father, my days are full, sometimes to the point of overflowing and chaotic. As I take a deep breath and begin this new day in prayer with You, please fill me with Your peace. Give me wisdom to create order in my life and to create space to breathe and think and especially focus on You. Guide me in the good works You want me to do, and direct me to the people You want me to serve. Amen.

> *"Peace I leave with you; my peace I give you. I do not give to you as the world gives. Do not let your hearts be troubled and do not be afraid."*
>
> JOHN 14:27 NIV

MY PRAYER FOR TODAY. . .

List the things in your life that seem to be stealing your peace. With God's wisdom, what changes can you make that will allow more of God's peace to fill you?

....

....

....

....

....

....

....

....

....

....

....

....

....

....

....

....

You will keep in perfect peace all who trust in you,
all whose thoughts are fixed on you! Trust in the
LORD always, for the LORD GOD is the eternal Rock.
ISAIAH 26:3–4 NLT

ANSWERS TO PRAYER. . .

MY PRAYER LIST. . .

Do not be anxious about anything, but in every situation,
by prayer and petition, with thanksgiving, present
your requests to God. And the peace of God,
which transcends all understanding, will guard
your hearts and your minds in Christ Jesus.
PHILIPPIANS 4:6–7 NIV

START WITH A PRAYER

Heavenly Father, I want songs of worship to You to always fill my mind. When I am in pain, help me to praise You. When I'm worried, help me to worship You. When I'm scared, help me to sing to You. No matter my need or the struggle I'm facing, or whatever blessing I'm receiving, I can cry out to You with requests, with thanksgiving, and with praise. May my words of honor and glory to You constantly overflow. Amen.

....

....

....

....

....

....

....

....

....

....

....

....

....

Come, let us sing to the Lord! Let us shout joyfully to the Rock of our salvation. Let us come to him with thanksgiving. Let us sing psalms of praise to him. For the Lord is a great God, a great King above all gods. He holds in his hands the depths of the earth and the mightiest mountains. The sea belongs to him, for he made it. His hands formed the dry land, too.

PSALM 95:1–5 NLT

MY PRAYER FOR TODAY. . .

Write down the lyrics to your favorite worship songs. Why do these words mean so much to you?

....

....

....

....

....

....

....

....

....

....

....

....

....

....

....

Let the message of Christ dwell among you richly as you teach and admonish one another with all wisdom through psalms, hymns, and songs from the Spirit, singing to God with gratitude in your hearts. And whatever you do, whether in word or deed, do it all in the name of the Lord Jesus, giving thanks to God the Father through him.
COLOSSIANS 3:16–17 NIV

ANSWERS TO PRAYER. . .

my PRAYER LiST. . .

*I will sing to the L*ORD *as long as I live; I will sing praise to my God while I have being.*
PSALM 104:33 ESV

START WITH A PRAYER

Heavenly Father, sometimes it seems the only thing I can do is groan to You because I feel overwhelmed—by the needs of others around me, by needs of my own, and by the sin that touches everything in this world. Encourage me with the truth that all of Your creation and all of Your believers are groaning as we wait for You, but we do so with great hope and with Your Holy Spirit helping us. We trust You are working all things out for good for those of us who love You and are called to Your purpose. Amen.

....

....

....

....

....

....

....

....

....

....

....

....

We know that all creation has been groaning as in the pains of childbirth right up to the present time. And we believers also groan, even though we have the Holy Spirit within us as a foretaste of future glory, for we long for our bodies to be released from sin and suffering. We, too, wait with eager hope for the day when God will give us our full rights as his adopted children, including the new bodies he has promised us. We were given this hope when we were saved. (If we already have something, we don't need to hope for it. But if we look forward to something we don't yet have, we must wait patiently and confidently.)

ROMANS 8:22–25 NLT

MY PRAYER FOR TODAY. . .

In what areas do you regularly struggle to know how to pray? How do you sense the Holy Spirit helping in your weakness and interceding for you in those areas that make you groan?

....

....

....

....

....

....

....

....

....

....

....

....

....

....

....

The Holy Spirit helps us in our weakness. For example, we don't know what God wants us to pray for. But the Holy Spirit prays for us with groanings that cannot be expressed in words. And the Father who knows all hearts knows what the Spirit is saying, for the Spirit pleads for us believers in harmony with God's own will.
ROMANS 8:26–27 NLT

ANSWERS TO PRAYER. . .

My PRAYER LiST. . .

....

....

....

....

....

....

....

....

....

....

....

....

....

....

....

....

....

*We know that God causes everything to work
together for the good of those who love God
and are called according to his purpose for them.*
ROMANS 8:28 NLT

START WITH A PRAYER

Heavenly Father, I praise and thank You for all Your compassion and comfort. You have shown them to me time and time again through so many different sources during every kind of suffering I've experienced. Remind me that You have comforted and cared for me so that I can in turn help comfort and care for others—and most of all point them to You as the Giver of it all. Amen.

*Praise be to the God and Father of our Lord Jesus Christ,
the Father of compassion and the God of all comfort, who
comforts us in all our troubles, so that we can comfort those in
any trouble with the comfort we ourselves receive from God.*
2 CORINTHIANS 1:3–4 NIV

MY PRAYER FOR TODAY. . .

Praise God for the ways He has shown you great comfort and care during suffering. Then describe how He has allowed you to be a source of comfort and care to others in their suffering.

....

....

....

....

....

....

....

....

....

....

....

....

....

....

....

....

Just as we share abundantly in the sufferings of Christ, so also our comfort abounds through Christ. If we are distressed, it is for your comfort and salvation; if we are comforted, it is for your comfort, which produces in you patient endurance of the same sufferings we suffer. And our hope for you is firm, because we know that just as you share in our sufferings, so also you share in our comfort.

2 CORINTHIANS 1:5–7 NIV

ANSWERS TO PRAYER. . .

MY PRAYER LIST. . .

....
....
....
....
....
....
....
....
....
....
....
....
....
....
....
....
....
....
....
....
....
....

*Shout for joy, you heavens; rejoice, you earth; burst
into song, you mountains! For the Lord comforts his
people and will have compassion on his afflicted ones.*
ISAIAH 49:13 NIV

START WITH A PRAYER

Heavenly Father, when my world seems turned upside down with unexpected change, please give me comfort, peace, and strength by reminding me that You never change. You have always been and always will be, and You are always good. Nothing in my life is a guaranteed constant except for You, Father. Thank You for being my strong Rock of security. No matter what happens, I know You will never leave or forsake me. Amen.

In the beginning you laid the foundations of the earth, and the heavens are the work of your hands. They will perish, but you remain; they will all wear out like a garment. Like clothing you will change them and they will be discarded. But you remain the same, and your years will never end.

PSALM 102:25–27 NIV

MY PRAYER FOR TODAY. . .

Describe a time of unexpected change in your life. How did God use it to show Himself as your unchanging security?

....

....

....

....

....

....

....

....

....

....

....

....

....

....

....

....

....

....

....

Jesus Christ is the same yesterday
and today and forever.
HEBREWS 13:8 NIV

ANSWERS TO PRAYER. . .

My PRAYER LiST. . .

....

....

....

....

....

....

....

....

....

....

....

....

....

....

....

....

....

....

....

....

*Whatever is good and perfect is a gift coming down to
us from God our Father, who created all the lights in the
heavens. He never changes or casts a shifting shadow.*
JAMES 1:17 NLT

START WITH A PRAYER

Heavenly Father, I want the strong women of faith featured in the Bible to inspire me. As I read about Anna, I want to focus on how she suffered tragedy but turned that into total devotion to You, staying in the temple and worshipping You with fasting and prayer. And then she was rewarded greatly by getting to see baby Jesus and know He was the expected Savior. If and when I suffer tragedy, please help me to draw closer to You and know You better like Anna did. Amen.

Anna, a prophet, was also there in the Temple. She was the daughter of Phanuel from the tribe of Asher, and she was very old. Her husband died when they had been married only seven years. Then she lived as a widow to the age of eighty-four. She never left the Temple but stayed there day and night, worshiping God with fasting and prayer. She came along just as Simeon was talking with Mary and Joseph, and she began praising God. She talked about the child to everyone who had been waiting expectantly for God to rescue Jerusalem.

LUKE 2:36–38 NLT

MY PRAYER FOR TODAY. . .

Describe the differences you've seen between people who turn away from God after a tragedy and people who draw closer to Him.

The Lord is near to the brokenhearted
and saves the crushed in spirit.
Psalm 34:18 esv

ANSWERS TO PRAYER. . .

MY PRAYER LIST. . .

....
....
....
....
....
....
....
....
....
....
....
....
....
....
....
....
....
....

No one is abandoned by the Lord forever. Though he brings grief, he also shows compassion because of the greatness of his unfailing love. For he does not enjoy hurting people or causing them sorrow.
LAMENTATIONS 3:31–33 NLT

START WITH A PRAYER

Heavenly Father, please help me to appreciate the good discipline You use to correct and guide me. Remind me that You are always loving me perfectly, even if I don't always enjoy what You're doing in my life. Show me how You are shaping me and teaching me and building character and endurance through good discipline. I love You and want to grow more like Jesus every day. Amen.

....

....

....

....

....

....

....

....

....

....

....

....

....

....

And have you forgotten the encouraging words God spoke to you as his children? He said, "My child, don't make light of the LORD's discipline, and don't give up when he corrects you. For the LORD disciplines those he loves, and he punishes each one he accepts as his child." As you endure this divine discipline, remember that God is treating you as his own children. Who ever heard of a child who is never disciplined by its father? If God doesn't discipline you as he does all of his children, it means that you are illegitimate and are not really his children at all. Since we respected our earthly fathers who disciplined us, shouldn't we submit even more to the discipline of the Father of our spirits, and live forever?

HEBREWS 12:5–9 NLT

MY PRAYER FOR TODAY. . .

What was your least favorite childhood discipline, and how did it shape your character? How have you seen God's discipline shaping your character? How have you thanked Him and honored Him because of that discipline?

....

....

....

....

....

....

....

....

....

....

....

....

....

....

....

....

No discipline is enjoyable while it is happening—
it's painful! But afterward there will be a peaceful
harvest of right living for those who are trained in this way.
HEBREWS 12:11 NLT

ANSWERS TO PRAYER. . .

MY PRAYER LiST. . .

_____

_____

_____

_____

_____

_____

_____

_____

_____

_____

_____

_____

_____

_____

_____

_____

_____

_____

_____

_____

_____

*My child, don't reject the Lord's discipline, and don't
be upset when he corrects you. For the Lord
corrects those he loves, just as a father
corrects a child in whom he delights.*
PROVERBS 3:11–12 NLT

START WITH A PRAYER

Heavenly Father, it's helpful that You acknowledged in your Word how hard it is to control everything I say. Please forgive me for the many mistakes I make with my tongue! Words are so powerful, and I want to constantly work to control mine. Help me speak words of praise to You and words of life, truth, and encouragement to others. Help me to not be careless or unkind with my words or engage in meaningless talk or spread gossip. Please help me get rid of any words that displease You. Amen.

We all make many mistakes. For if we could control our tongues, we would be perfect and could also control ourselves in every other way. We can make a large horse go wherever we want by means of a small bit in its mouth. And a small rudder makes a huge ship turn wherever the pilot chooses to go, even though the winds are strong. In the same way, the tongue is a small thing that makes grand speeches. But a tiny spark can set a great forest on fire. And among all the parts of the body, the tongue is a flame of fire. It is a whole world of wickedness, corrupting your entire body. It can set your whole life on fire, for it is set on fire by hell itself. People can tame all kinds of animals, birds, reptiles, and fish, but no one can tame the tongue. It is restless and evil, full of deadly poison. Sometimes it praises our Lord and Father, and sometimes it curses those who have been made in the image of God. And so blessing and cursing come pouring out of the same mouth. Surely, my brothers and sisters, this is not right!

JAMES 3:2–10 NLT

MY PRAYER FOR TODAY. . .

How can having more conversations with God in prayer help you have more self-control over your conversations with others?

....

....

....

....

....

....

....

....

....

....

....

....

....

....

....

....

....

....

....

Set a guard, O Lᴏʀᴅ, over my mouth;
keep watch over the door of my lips!
Psᴀʟᴍ 141:3 ᴇsᴠ

ANSWERS TO PRAYER. . .

MY PRAYER LIST. . .

Do not let any unwholesome talk come out of your mouths,
but only what is helpful for building others up according
to their needs, that it may benefit those who listen.
EPHESIANS 4:29 NIV

START WITH A PRAYER

*Heavenly Father, when I feel rejected, remind me how hated
and rejected Your Son was—so rejected that people beat Him
and then crucified Him. But thankfully that wasn't the end.
In Christ's rejection and suffering, You were working to offer
eternal salvation. Remind me that You are working in ways
I don't know yet when I am rejected and suffering too. Please
comfort me and strengthen my faith as You work behind
the scenes and prepare great rewards in heaven! Amen.*

....

....

....

....

....

....

....

....

....

....

....

....

"God blesses you when people mock you and persecute you and lie about you and say all sorts of evil things against you because you are my followers. Be happy about it! Be very glad! For a great reward awaits you in heaven. And remember, the ancient prophets were persecuted in the same way."
MATTHEW 5:11–12 NLT

MY PRAYER FOR TODAY. . .

....

....

....

....

....

....

....

....

....

....

....

....

....

....

....

....

....

....

....

....

....

Describe ways you have suffered or been rejected for following Jesus. How has God strengthened and encouraged you because of what you've experienced?

....

....

....

....

....

....

....

....

....

....

....

....

....

....

....

....

....

....

He was despised and rejected by mankind, a man of suffering, and familiar with pain. Like one from whom people hide their faces he was despised, and we held him in low esteem.

Isaiah 53:3 NIV

ANSWERS TO PRAYER. . .

MY PRAYER LIST. . .

Consider him who endured such opposition from sinners,
so that you will not grow weary and lose heart.
HEBREWS 12:3 NIV

START WITH A PRAYER

Heavenly Father, thank You so much that You never get tired of hearing from me. Jesus taught that You want me to be persistent in prayer. You want me to keep seeking You. No one else could ever truly claim not to get tired of listening to others sometimes, but You can! You never grow weary, God, and I am so grateful. Thank You for caring about every one of my requests and needs and concerns. Amen.

Then, teaching them more about prayer, he used this story: "Suppose you went to a friend's house at midnight, wanting to borrow three loaves of bread. You say to him, 'A friend of mine has just arrived for a visit, and I have nothing for him to eat.' And suppose he calls out from his bedroom, 'Don't bother me. The door is locked for the night, and my family and I are all in bed. I can't help you.' But I tell you this—though he won't do it for friendship's sake, if you keep knocking long enough, he will get up and give you whatever you need because of your shameless persistence. And so I tell you, keep on asking, and you will receive what you ask for. Keep on seeking, and you will find. Keep on knocking, and the door will be opened to you. For everyone who asks, receives. Everyone who seeks, finds. And to everyone who knocks, the door will be opened."

LUKE 11:5–10 NLT

MY PRAYER FOR TODAY. . .

....
....
....
....
....
....
....
....
....
....
....
....
....
....
....
....
....
....
....
....
....

Which of your prayer requests and concerns do you sometimes wonder if God grows tired of hearing? How does Jesus' teaching in Luke 11 encourage you in them?

....

....

....

....

....

....

....

....

....

....

....

....

....

....

....

"You fathers—if your children ask for a fish, do you give them a snake instead? Or if they ask for an egg, do you give them a scorpion? Of course not! So if you sinful people know how to give good gifts to your children, how much more will your heavenly Father give the Holy Spirit to those who ask him."

LUKE 11:11–13 NLT

ANSWERS TO PRAYER. . .

MY PRAYER LIST. . .

So let us come boldly to the throne of our gracious God.
There we will receive his mercy, and we will find
grace to help us when we need it most.
HEBREWS 4:16 NLT

START WITH A PRAYER

Dear God, I pray to and praise You in multiple ways and places, sometimes with spoken words, sometimes just with my thoughts, sometimes with singing, sometimes with written words. Help me to remember that You speak to Your people through anything You want, sometimes in big dramatic ways like the burning bush with Moses and sometimes in quiet ways like a gentle whisper with Elijah. No matter how You speak to me, Father, I want to be listening for You and obeying You! Amen.

....

....

....

....

....

....

....

....

....

....

....

....

"Go out and stand before me on the mountain," the LORD told him. And as Elijah stood there, the LORD passed by, and a mighty windstorm hit the mountain. It was such a terrible blast that the rocks were torn loose, but the LORD was not in the wind. After the wind there was an earthquake, but the LORD was not in the earthquake. And after the earthquake there was a fire, but the LORD was not in the fire. And after the fire there was the sound of a gentle whisper. When Elijah heard it, he wrapped his face in his cloak and went out and stood at the entrance of the cave. And a voice said, "What are you doing here, Elijah?"
1 KINGS 19:11–13 NLT

MY PRAYER FOR TODAY. . .

Do you have favorite times and places to offer prayer and praises to God? Describe them and why they are your favorite.

....
....
....
....
....
....
....
....
....
....
....
....
....
....
....
....
....
....

But Jesus often withdrew to lonely places and prayed.
LUKE 5:16 NIV

ANSWERS TO PRAYER. . .

My PRAYER LiST. . .

....

....

....

....

....

....

....

....

....

....

....

....

....

....

....

....

....

....

....

....

....

....

*I lift up my eyes to the hills. From where does
my help come? My help comes from the
Lord, who made heaven and earth.*
PSALM 121:1-2 ESV

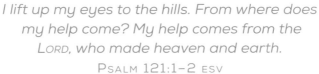

START WITH A PRAYER

Heavenly Father, when I am growing tired of coming to You in prayer, sometimes with seemingly no answers or results, remind me that You are always listening and working and answering even if I cannot see or sense what You are doing. You strive to give justice to Your people. Help me to continue to cry out to You every single day and night. I love You, and I am so grateful for the privilege of prayer! Amen.

One day Jesus told his disciples a story to show that they should always pray and never give up. "There was a judge in a certain city," he said, "who neither feared God nor cared about people. A widow of that city came to him repeatedly, saying, 'Give me justice in this dispute with my enemy.' The judge ignored her for a while, but finally he said to himself, 'I don't fear God or care about people, but this woman is driving me crazy. I'm going to see that she gets justice, because she is wearing me out with her constant requests!'" Then the Lord said, "Learn a lesson from this unjust judge. Even he rendered a just decision in the end. So don't you think God will surely give justice to his chosen people who cry out to him day and night? Will he keep putting them off? I tell you, he will grant justice to them quickly! But when the Son of Man returns, how many will he find on the earth who have faith?"

LUKE 18:1–8 NLT

MY PRAYER FOR TODAY. . .

Describe a time when you were tempted to give up on prayer. How did God lead you back to Him during that time?

....

....

....

....

....

....

....

....

....

....

....

....

....

....

....

....

....

....

Rejoice always, pray without ceasing, give thanks in all circumstances; for this is the will of God in Christ Jesus for you.
1 THESSALONIANS 5:16–18 ESV

ANSWERS TO PRAYER. . .

MY PRAYER LIST. . .

But Jesus looked at them and said, "With man this
is impossible, but with God all things are possible."
MATTHEW 19:26 ESV

START WITH A PRAYER

Heavenly Father, I long for the day when Your Son returns and You establish the new heaven and earth where righteousness dwells forever. Remind me that You are never moving too slowly. You are so loving, Father. You want no one to perish but rather all to repent and accept Your Son as Savior. I praise You for Your goodness and patience, and I trust in Your perfect timing. Help me live my life to serve and honor You as I look forward to that glorious day of Your coming. Amen.

But do not forget this one thing, dear friends: With the Lord a day is like a thousand years, and a thousand years are like a day. The Lord is not slow in keeping his promise, as some understand slowness. Instead he is patient with you, not wanting anyone to perish, but everyone to come to repentance. But the day of the Lord will come like a thief. The heavens will disappear with a roar; the elements will be destroyed by fire, and the earth and everything done in it will be laid bare. Since everything will be destroyed in this way, what kind of people ought you to be? You ought to live holy and godly lives as you look forward to the day of God and speed its coming.

2 PETER 3:8–12 NIV

MY PRAYER FOR TODAY. . .

What mix of emotions do you feel as you focus on and pray for the day of the Lord?

....

....

....

....

....

....

....

....

....

....

....

....

....

....

....

....

That day will bring about the destruction of the heavens by fire, and the elements will melt in the heat. But in keeping with his promise we are looking forward to a new heaven and a new earth, where righteousness dwells.

2 PETER 3:12–13 NIV

ANSWERS TO PRAYER. . .

MY PRAYER LIST. . .

Grow in the grace and knowledge of our Lord
and Savior Jesus Christ. To him be glory
both now and forever! Amen.
2 PETER 3:18 NIV

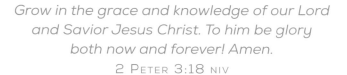

More Prayer Life Inspiration for the Entire Family!

The Prayer Map for Men
978-1-64352-438-2

The Prayer Map for Women
978-1-68322-557-7

The Prayer Map for Girls
978-1-68322-559-1

The Prayer Map for Boys
978-1-68322-558-4

The Prayer Map for Teens
978-1-68322-556-0

These purposeful prayer journals are a fun and creative way to more fully experience the power of prayer. Each page guides you to write out thoughts, ideas, and lists. . .which then creates a specific "map" for you to follow as you talk to God. Each map includes a spot to record the date, so you can look back on your prayers and see how God has worked in your life. *The Prayer Map* will not only encourage you to spend time talking with God about the things that matter most. . .it will also help you build a healthy spiritual habit of continual prayer for life!
Spiral Bound / $7.99